Budgeting for Beginners

M.L. HUMPHREY

CONTENTS

CONTENTS (CONT.)

CONTENTS (CONT.)

INTRODUCTION

This book is meant to help you get a handle on your personal finances. It's for beginners who've never really had to sit down before and think these things through.

When I wrote the book I asked myself how I approach these things. What information do I need? How do I assess that information? And what do I do once I know where I stand?

Those questions are what are behind the three main sections of this book.

In the first section of the book we're going to walk through how to determine what you earn, what you spend, what you own, and what you owe. That's the information you need to start managing your money better and work towards your financial goals. If you don't know where you are, you can't get to where you need to go.

In that section I also spend time talking about how to judge these things if your income is not steady and predictable or not paid out monthly. So if you're self-employed, a student whose main income comes from lump-sum payments, your income is commission-based, or your hours are unpredictable. We'll walk through how to determine what you earn when you're in a situation like that.

We'll also discuss in some detail the difference between what something is worth on paper and what it's really worth when you need it. (A very important distinction for some of us.)

Next we'll move into the second section of the book where we talk about what to do with those numbers. How do you compare them to one another? When do you know that you're on track and when should you start to worry?

Finally, in the third section we'll walk through strategies for improving now that you know where you stand and where your weaknesses might be.

In an ideal world we'd all be debt-free, maxing out our 401(k), and with a six-month cash reserve. But that's not most people's reality. Most people are barely stumbling from paycheck to paycheck. This book is meant to help you get a handle on things so that you're not stumbling along, so that you have a direction and a way to improve your situation.

Now, a quick word of caution before we start: This book involves math. Not complex math. We're not going to do any calculus. But you are going to need to do some addition, subtraction, multiplication, and division. There's no way around it. I'll walk you through everything you need to know, so just stick with me and you'll be fine. But I wanted to warn you up front.

(And if you're shaky on basic math, that's fine. That's life. But you should probably brush up on your math before you start this book. There's no way to implement what we're going to talk about here without being able to do addition, subtraction, multiplication, and division. I did write a companion guide for the first version of this book, Juggling Your Finances: Basic Math Primer, that covers that, but there are plenty of free resources out there as well.)

Also, for those of you who learn better listening than reading, the basic content covered in this book is available in audio as *The Juggling Your Finances Starter Kit*.

Okay then. Let's get started.

GETTING STARTED:
EARN SPEND OWN
OWE

WHAT DO YOU EARN?

The first thing you need to know if you're going to get a handle on your finances is what you earn. In other words, what cash do you have coming in that you can use to pay your bills?

That requires that you choose a timeframe for tracking this information.

I tend to do all my budgeting on a monthly basis. Most of my bills, like rent, utilities, phone, internet, and credit card, are billed on a monthly basis, so it makes sense to me to also track my income on a monthly basis so I can match the two together.

Most people get paid more than once a month, but since expenses are often monthly I think tracking income monthly makes the most sense. It lets you compare apples to apples, so to speak.

From here on out we're going to talk about tracking income (what you earn) and expenses (what you pay) on a monthly basis. But if it makes more sense for you to use a different time period, then do so. The same principles apply no matter the time period involved.

Your goal is to know what you bring in for a specific time period and compare that to what you have to pay out for the same time period.

So, what do you earn in a month?

Salaried Jobs

For those with steady salaried jobs, this is pretty easy to calculate.

Look at the automatic deposits or paystubs from your employer for the last month and add them up. If you get paid $563.42 every two weeks, then your monthly income is $1,126.84.

Note that the number that matters here is NOT what your gross pay is.

(That's the amount you're paid before they take out taxes.)

What we care about is your net pay. (What you actually take home.)

In other words, it doesn't matter if you earn $24,000 a year. What matters is that you actually take home $18,480 a year.

(Note that I made those numbers up. The percentage of your gross income that you take home will depend on your income and what you have to pay in taxes. In the U.S. that's related to how many deductions you claim when you fill out your tax form. Two people can earn the exact same amount on a gross basis and be paid very different amounts depending upon their deductions. So, use *your* actual numbers for this.)

Why do we care about net pay instead of gross pay?

Because that's the money you can actually spend each month.

Now, one quick comment here and then we'll move on to the more tricky situations.

I used to work for an employer that paid every two weeks. I think it was every other Friday. In that case, I actually received 26 paychecks per year, which means that two months of every year I received three paychecks instead of two.

If you're in that position, only count the amount you receive in two paychecks for monthly budgeting purposes.

Treat those extra two paychecks as a bonus that you can put towards something special.

Why?

Because you won't actually have that money available to you each month. And odds are you aren't going to take those extra checks and parcel them out over the other months in the year.

If you're anything like most of us, cash in hand is cash to spend. You won't remember to keep back $500 per month for the next five months. You'll see $2,500 and think that you can buy that flat screen TV after all.

So, fine. Treat that third check twice a year as bonus money.

This is especially important to pay attention to when you get a new job.

The job I had that paid that way was my first job right out of college. I didn't even realize when I accepted the job that what I was going to earn each month wasn't really 1/12 of my salary. Fortunately I was able to pay my bills based upon the amount I was receiving each month, but it could've been a big wake-up call for me if I'd been living just a little bit closer to the line.

This is also something to think about if you're ever offered two jobs at once. Maybe they pay the same, but if you need the full salary to live on, take the job that pays twice a month instead of every two weeks. If you don't really need the full salary and have difficulty saving for big purchases, take the job that pays every two weeks because it's a bit like being forced to save 8% of your income every year.

Bottom line here: If you're salaried, the amount you get paid each and every month is the amount you should use for budgeting purposes.

Hourly Jobs

Not everyone has a salaried job. Many people work jobs that pay hourly. And it's not always clear how many hours you're going to get week-to-week.

If you work for a good employer, they'll try to keep it steady, but sometimes that's just not possible. I worked summer entertainment jobs and we occasionally had big weekends where I'd work twelve hour days four days in a row. That would be followed by an off weekend where I only worked two eight-hour shifts.

In this case, you need to determine a reasonable income that you expect to earn each and every month.

If work is reasonably steady you can just use the average hours you work every month. If not, you'll have to take a different approach.

When I worked those entertainment jobs, we had a big weekend in May, July, and September. That means June and August were months with lower hours.

If I'd taken an average of May's hours and tried to estimate what I was going to earn in June, I'd have been in trouble.

What you want if you're in a situation like this is a number that you can count on every single month, not some pie in the sky dream amount that you really hope and pray you'll get. (Hope doesn't pay bills. And promises that you'll pay next month don't stop the bounced check fees.)

That means leave out those big bonus weekends or overtime pay unless you consistently get them every month.

And, once again, you want the amount you'll take home, not the amount you'll gross.

Which means that however many hours you think you'll work, you need to then take out an amount for taxes. If you've already been paid by the company, you can look at an old pay stub and see the difference between what you grossed ($10/hour for 10 hours is $100) versus what you were paid ($100 minus 23% for taxes is $77).

Use that percentage to calculate what you can expect to take home. (100%-23% means you take home 77% of your gross pay.)

As a quick example: Let's say you think that, on average, you'll work 25 hours a week. Your pay is $10/hour. And you generally pay about 23% of each paycheck to taxes. Then the amount you can expect to earn each month is $770. (4 weeks*25 hours*10 dollar per hour*.77 to account for taxes.)

Find the amount you can rely on. And if you can't rely on an amount, then you may have to do what some people, like me, do, and not include an income in your budget at all. I instead focus on how many months of expenses I can cover with the cash I have available. (More on that later.)

Generally, if you do have a job that pays hourly you know that you'll at least work X hours each month and can use that to budget with.

Bonuses

If a large percentage of your pay comes from bonuses, this can be very tricky. There are jobs out there where the bonus paid is large multiples of the employee's income. (Think investment banking or sales jobs.)

And sometimes bonuses can make your income "chunky" (for lack of a better word).

You're going along earning $2,000 a month in salary and then each quarter you receive a large payment of $6,000. If the bulk of your income comes from these periodic payments and you can't predict what they'll be ahead of time, it makes it hard to budget.

Your best bet would be to budget as if the bonuses don't exist. Just budget using your salary amount. But for many people a bonus is too large a part of their income to do that.

So a few things to consider when it comes to bonuses.

First, you need to understand that the percentage you'll pay to taxes on that bonus is probably going to be higher than what you pay for your salary. Basically, expect to take home a smaller percentage of a bonus than you would a normal paycheck. (Assuming the bonus is a higher number than your normal paycheck.) I used to just use 50% as an estimate and be pleasantly surprised when I brought home 60% instead.

Second, you need to evaluate the real nature of the bonus and decide if it's reliable enough and predictable enough for you to include the bonus in your budget.

I've had two different jobs that used bonuses. One I was able to include in my budgeting, the other I wasn't.

The first job paid an hourly wage and a bonus for every service I booked. Both the wage and bonus were paid every two weeks and I knew at the end of each shift (if I bothered to check) what my bonus was going to be for that day.

We were also selling a service where people called in to us and where almost every caller bought the service, so it was just a question of how many calls I handled in a given hour and which service they bought.

After a few weeks, I had a pretty good feel for things. My base salary was $6/hr, but with call-ins I was consistently earning $10/hr. Sure, sometimes I earned close to $20/hr, but I almost always earned $10/hr.

For budgeting purposes, I was comfortable estimating my income from that job at $10/hr.

The key here is to use a number you can *reasonably expect* to receive for the time period. It's not to assume that you'll hit a home run every time. It's to know that most times at bat, you hit a solid single.

I'm going to start sounding redundant here, but plan for what's reasonable. Don't budget based on wishes and dreams.

The second job I had that paid a bonus was a salaried job. It paid a bonus once a year. The bonus could be anything. Some years, some people in our office didn't even receive a bonus. In other years, someone might receive a 10% bonus and the guy sitting next to them might receive a 50% bonus and you never knew if you'd be the 10% guy or the 50% guy.

There were also no clear, objective criteria used to determine bonuses, so even if you thought you'd had a good year, you really didn't know what that meant for your bonus.

Which didn't keep me from preparing a little grid of possible outcomes based upon my prior year's bonus percentage. I would list my salary and then generate a range of options both higher and lower than the prior year's bonus percent to see what I might get and mentally spend that money on whatever it was I wanted that year.

But I didn't use that bonus as part of my monthly budget.

And until I was told what my bonus was going to be, that bonus was zero as far as my spending was concerned. There was no guarantee I'd even receive the bonus, so I just acted as if it didn't exist until the money was actually in my account.

Do not count on a bonus like that. That's the road to heartache. Because what happens if there is no bonus that year?

Or if the bonus is far less than you'd thought it would be? You're screwed.

Your best bet with annual bonuses like that is to ignore them.

Remember, we're talking about estimating your monthly *income* here. Once you get paid, the bonus becomes part of what you own and you can offset that money against your expenses and know that you've got enough to cover X months.

But for estimating income? Pretend it doesn't exist.

So bottom line: If you're paid a bonus that is easy to predict, occurs on a consistent and regular basis, and pays out often enough to include in your income (weekly, bi-weekly, or monthly), then you can include an estimated bonus amount in your income. If you're paid a bonus that only occurs once a year, isn't guaranteed, or isn't easy to predict, then don't include it as part of your income.

Seasonally Variable Income

It gets much harder to budget if you're in a profession where the income varies throughout the year. This often happens with sales jobs where the product you're selling is more popular in one season versus another. It can also apply to many self-employed individuals.

My father was in a couple of fields like this.

He was a self-employed accountant, which meant that a substantial portion of his income came from that three months around tax time.

He was also a sign salesman and, for whatever reason, most companies buy signage in the summer months.

I also found with consulting that I earned 80% of my income in six months of the year. Maybe something to do with fiscal planning for large companies, but after three or four years of self-employment, I could pretty much guess when projects would come along.

Now, how you handle this will depend on what your income looks like.

For my dad, with both the sign sales and accounting, he did have year-round work, so he had a baseline income he could pretty much count on month-to month. This is the number he could use for budgeting.

Those high sales months when he earned more? Bonus money. Not used for day-to-day expenses.

What you don't want to do in a situation like this is have bills that are more than your steady and reliable income and tell yourself that you'll catch up when the high season hits.

So, say you generally earn $2,500 every month, but some months you earn as much as $5,000 a month. Just use $2,500 for budgeting purposes, because that's the amount you can be almost certain you'll earn month in and month out.

But that's not how it works for everyone. Some people have zero-income months followed by high-income months.

That's how consulting was for me. I'd have months that were so close to zero they didn't even count as income followed by very high income months.

If you have that kind of income pattern, you have to be very good at saving money from the good times to cover the bad times because NOTHING is coming in during the bad times.

If you find yourself in a situation like that, assume your monthly income is zero.

I know. That seems hard to swallow. You know you make money some months. GOOD money.

But it's not predictable enough to treat like a steady income.

As I mentioned with the hourly wage example above, if you can't predict your monthly income, you have to assume it'll be zero.

What you then do is compare your monthly expenses to the cash you have in the bank to figure out how many months of expenses you can cover without additional income.

And when you drop below your "panic level" you take steps to get more money in the door. Whether that's doing temp work, drumming up more business, or taking a salaried job, it doesn't matter. You need money and soon.

For me, every time I got to the point where I had less than three months' of expenses in the bank, I started to sweat and look for alternatives. I knew I needed more cash coming in the door in the next three months or I wouldn't be able to pay my bills and I knew it would take about a month to find a project and at least six weeks to get paid after I had.

You need to look at your own situation and decide based upon the type of work you do and how long it takes to get paid for that work how many months you need to keep in reserve. Your panic point is unique to your circumstances.

Okay, so bottom line for seasonally variable work: if you

have a steady and reliable amount of money coming in every month, then use that income number in your budget.

If your income isn't steady and reliable month-to-month, then count your income as zero and use the "how many months of expenses do I have in savings" approach instead.

Do not, under either scenario, use the average of your income for the year. It'll get you in trouble because you will have months where you don't earn that number.

And when those months happen, if you're right at the edge with your expenses, you will miss payments. That will ruin your credit and cost you money you don't need to spend on things like bounced check fees, payday loans, or overdraft fees. Not to mention the cost of having a low credit score. Don't do it.

Spot Work or Cash Payments

Some people earn most of their income through spot work or cash-based work. Things like housesitting, dog walking, day labor, etc.

This category covers anything that pays in cash and isn't consistent.

(If it's consistent, then I'd treat it like hourly work above without the cut for taxes. Although this is where I should point out to you that just because you get paid cash and no one takes out taxes doesn't mean you don't owe taxes on that income. But that's between you and your government.)

With cash work, even though the amount of work you get might vary from week to week or month to month, it may be possible to figure out an average income for the month.

Just as above, is there an amount you can *reasonably expect* to earn every month? If so, include that amount as income in your budgeting.

If you have no clue month-to-month what you're going to earn, then as with the scenarios above, you need to list your income as zero and instead compare your expenses to your savings. And again, as above, you'll want to calculate how many months of expenses you can cover with the cash you have in the bank and figure out your panic level. At what point do you need to scramble for more money?

It's possible that someone in this situation has no cash in the bank and is working on a cash basis just to put groceries on the table week-to-week. Don't stress if that's you, although ideally we want to get you to a point where that's not what you're doing.

Remember, right now we're just getting a handle on where you stand so we can find ways to improve your situation. If you don't earn money consistently enough to count as monthly income and don't have any savings, still list your income as zero and we'll figure out strategies for dealing with that once we have the whole picture.

Pension/Social Security/Disability/Stipend Payments

Generally, pension, social security, and disability payments are paid once a month. Stipend payments are often once a quarter.

They work much the same way that salary payments do because they're consistent and predictable. My dad's social security payments arrived on the third of the month every month and in the same amount.

For pension, social security, and disability payment recipients, include the amount you receive every month as income in your budget.

For stipend recipients, you may want to budget quarterly. Or you may want to do what I've told others to do above and treat your monthly income as zero and instead compare your monthly expenses to the balance you have in your bank accounts. And consider pre-paying your bills when you get the money. Better to pay three months of rent in advance than not have a roof over your head in month three.

Other

It just occurred to me that there might still be some sources of income I hadn't covered yet. Like alimony. Or client payments for the self-employed.

I was fortunate with my consulting that my client paid like clockwork on the fifteenth of each month, so when I was on a long-term project I could estimate a monthly income amount.

Some ex-spouses pay alimony on time, too.

But then there are those others…The ones that can't be relied upon to pay on time. (Clients and exes.)

If you think the income is steady and reliable month-to-month, include it in your income.

If you can't predict from one month to the next what you're going to receive, then list the value as zero when you're calculating your income and instead use the approach of comparing your monthly expenses to your cash in the bank.

Bottom line of this exercise is to figure out how much you can *reasonably expect* to receive each month.

Again, this isn't about dreaming or hoping or praying.

This is what you realistically earn. What do you actually bring home each month on a regular and consistent basis?

That's the number you want to use to compare to how much you spend each month.

In an ideal world, the amount you earn each month will be more than the amount you pay out each month.

But sometimes that's not the case. That doesn't mean you're going bankrupt or that you aren't managing your finances properly. It just means you need to approach your finances a little differently.

(Although if you're spending more than you're earning and you know that you don't have other sources of money coming in soon and that your income and expenses are steady month-to month, you need to be worried. Because that's a losing scenario.)

Don't worry yet. We're just getting the numbers together at this point.

Or if you're looking good, don't gloat yet.

Just because you can pay your current bills every month, doesn't mean you're on track. You're staying above water, sure. But you may not be prepared to handle an emergency, like losing your job. And you may not be able to meet your longer-term goals like buying a house or paying for your kids' education.

Okay, next step in figuring out where you stand is calculating how much you pay out each month.

WHAT DO YOU SPEND?

Whatever time period you decided to use for your income, you should also use for calculating what you pay out. So I'm sticking with one month.

Alright, then. How much do you spend in a month?

Let's start with the easy numbers to calculate:

• What is your rent or mortgage payment?

• What do you pay for internet every month?

• What do you pay for your car?

• What do you pay for your car insurance? (Some plans have you pay every year or every six months. If you're struggling with finances, it may be better to move to a monthly payment plan so you can better align your payments with your income.)

• What do you pay for health insurance?

• What do you pay for student loans?

• What do you pay for utilities like water and electricity every month?

• What do you pay for your phone?

Most of the payments above are pretty stable month-to-month. Rent and mortgage payments are generally fixed for twelve months or the lease term if that's shorter. Car payments are also generally fixed. Car insurance and health insurance generally stay the same for a year. As do student loans and internet.

Now, utilities and phone may vary. Gas and heat bills can skyrocket in the winter months if you have to run your furnace a lot. Water bills can sometimes be high in the summer if you have a lawn to water. Your best bet if you haven't done so yet and are living close to the edge is to get your utility company to do standardized billing year-round. They charge you more in the down months and less in the high months, but it helps to know that you owe $125 a month every month for utilities instead of $60 one month and $200 another.

If you can't find a way to make your bill consistent month-to-month, you can take one of two approaches:

First, you can try to use an average expense. Maybe a three-month average for that particular bill or, if you have bills from prior years, the average for that month for that bill for the prior three years.

Problem with this approach is that the amount in your budget is going to change month-to-month.

The second option is to use a number that's close to the highest amount you pay per month. So, for example, when I had a house I'd pay anywhere from $75 to $150 for electric and gas each month. My budget listed that expense as $125. In the $75 months, I was pleasantly surprised. In the $150 months, I wasn't killed by the extra $25.

The goal here is to assign a value to each expense that is what you normally and consistently pay for that expense.

And to err on the high side so that you're never blindsided.

Now, note what I left out of that original list: Credit card, gas, groceries, entertainment, and other discretionary spending.

First, if you have a credit card with a balance and you don't pay it off every month, include the amount you pay to the card in the numbers above. (Ideally, this number will be more than the minimum payment on the card. Right now we're just trying to figure out where you are, but paying the minimum on a credit card is a good way to ensure that everything you bought on that card ends up costing you ten times what you thought you paid for it.)

Next, we need to know what you spend on everything else every month. Gas, groceries, your bar tab, shopping, Starbucks lattes, gambling, etc.

Depending on how you handle your finances, this will be really easy to do or really hard.

I tend to use my credit card for almost all of my discretionary expenses. Basically, anything that isn't a set payment goes on my credit card. I then pay off the credit card at the end of each month.

(A reason some people recommend you don't use a credit card in this way is because people use their credit card but then can't pay it off so end up just more in debt than before. Putting all those expenses on a credit card requires either discipline enough to keep your spending within your budget or it requires enough income to be able to cover whatever you happen to charge that month.)

Because I use my credit card and not cash, I know what I spend my money on each month. I can take that credit card statement and add up the amounts and put them into their appropriate categories.

If you pay cash for things and don't keep the receipts, you're going to have a gigantic black hole in your expenses.

You can add up your ATM withdrawals to know that you spent $600 cash last month, but on what? Coffee? Food? Beer? Loans to friends? Who knows?

Until you track and document your cash spending, you aren't going to know where you spend that money. So start saving receipts. Or write it down in a notebook. Whatever you do, get a handle on where you spend your cash.

And just because you don't spend the same amount every day, week, or month doesn't mean you can't budget for it. You just need to use averages to do so.

How? Well, ideally, you want to have about three months of expenses to look at.

For each category where you consistently spend money, add it to your budget using the average of the last three months. (If you had some extraordinary one-off expenses during those three months, don't include those amounts in these categories. Move them to miscellaneous.)

For example, I have categories for food, gas, and travel.

I also have a catch-all entry for Miscellaneous, because I don't know what I'll buy each month, but I know I'll end up having to pay for something I don't normally buy like an oil change or friend's birthday present.

Try to include everything you spend somewhere in your budget. At the end of the day, this is what you want to know:

• What do you spend your money on each month? (This is what you pay each month plus anything you charge on a credit card)

• What amount of money do you need each month to pay your expenses? (This will differ from 1 if you're charging things but not paying off your credit card each month.)

You will likely have times in your life when you're spending more money each month than you're paying out each month. Those are the times when you're using debt, like credit cards, to finance your daily life.

I had to do that in college.

And some people have to do it when they lose their jobs. The kids still have to be fed, after all.

Just know that you can't do that long-term. And the more you do it, the bigger the hole you're going to have to dig yourself out of. What you want to be careful about is using credit card debt to buy crap like electronics and music and games and things like that when you have no long-term plan or vision for ever paying for it.

That is how you screw yourself over.

Don't do it.

Alright. So now that we know what you spend each month, what do you own?

WHAT DO YOU OWN?

In finance circles this is sometimes phrased as "what are your assets"?

The first step in determining what you have is to list everything you own.

- Do you have any bank accounts? Checking? Savings?

- Do you have a home? (Even if it has a mortgage on it, still list it.)

- Do you have a car? (Same as above. If you have a car loan, still list the car as something you own.)

- What about a retirement account? Do you have a 401(k) through work? Or an IRA?

- What about a 529 plan for education?

- What about a brokerage or investment account?

- What about any valuable collections? Like comic books or dolls or something?

- What about your possessions? Do you own that 50" TV in your front room?

• Are you owed money for work you've already performed? (For example, as a self-published writer, Amazon owes me money for books I sold two months ago because they don't pay for sales right away.)

Once you've listed everything you own, the next step is to assign a value to each of those items.

This is where things start to get tricky, so we'll walk through the list one item at a time

For each one, I want you to create two columns: Value and Liquidated Value. Value is what people will tell you something is worth. Liquidated Value is what you can realistically get for it.

As you can guess, I care (and you should care) more about liquidated value.

For example, if you look up your retirement account right now, you'll see a balance in that account. But that's not the value you'll receive if you actually try to get that money right now.

You may not even be able to access that money if it's at your current employer. If you can access it, you'll probably have to pay taxes and penalties.

We'll track both values, because paper value can be meaningful when you're trying to decide if you've saved enough for retirement or the kids' educations, but for any immediate financial needs you really only care about liquidated value.

Okay. Let's walk through every type of account:

Checking Account

This one should be simple. Take the balance in the account and subtract any outstanding payments that you've made that have yet to clear.

For example, if you have $1,500 in your account, but you wrote a rent check for $1,200 yesterday, then you'd list the value of this account as $300, because you've already spent that $1,200. No getting it back now. And if you forget that you wrote that check and spend more than the $300 you have left, you're going to bounce your rent check.

Not something you want to do.

So your balance in the checking account is the current balance minus any outstanding check payments or debit payments.

(Be careful with debit payments because they don't always hit your account immediately. For example, if you pay for gas on Saturday with your bank card the real amount you paid may not show in the account until Monday. It's an easy and ugly way to overdraw your account if you then buy something on Sunday, because it'll look like you have enough money in your account when you really don't. One of the reasons I don't use a bank card. I use a credit card instead, so I don't have a nasty surprise like that mid-month.)

The value and liquidated value of your checking account should be the same number. It's cash in hand.

Savings Account

This one will usually be just the account balance.

If you have a true savings account you're not really allowed to make more than three withdrawals in a month, so you shouldn't need to make adjustments for outstanding checks or debit card payments.

But if you do have pending checks or debit card payments, do make those adjustments.

For a basic savings account at your bank, the value and the liquidated value should be the same as the balance in the account.

If you have money in Certificates of Deposit (CDs) or something like that, then you're going to have to adjust the liquidated value. Let's talk about those separately.

Certificates of Deposit

Some people, invest their savings in certificates of deposit or CDs. Basically, the way a CD works is that in exchange for agreeing to let the bank hold your money for a set period of time, they agree to pay you more than a savings account pays.

(These can be very useful if interest rates are high. For example, if you have enough in the bank to cover six months of expenses, putting your money into a CD can be a nice way to earn a little extra money while your money is sitting there. You can set them up so that one month's worth of expenses is coming due each month in case you end up needing the funds. It's called laddering, I believe.)

Problem with CDs is that you agree to lock up that money for a set period of time. The longer the period of time, the more they pay you. But if you need that money before the time period is up, you pay a penalty for an early withdrawal.

That means that for CDs the value and the liquidated value will be different.

In the value column, put whatever the statement balance is for the CDs. In the liquidated value column, list the statement balance minus any penalties and fees you'll have to pay to get to the money this month.

Let's do an example:

You have a six-month CD for $5,000. The early penalty withdrawal is a flat $250. (I'm making this up. If you ever do buy a CD, read the fine print to know what it'll cost you to pull that money early and decide for yourself if the interest they're paying you is worth it.)

Okay, so the value of your CD is $5,000.

The liquidated value of your CD is $5,000 minus $250. Or $4,750.

If you're in money troubles, guess which number you care about? The number you will actually get to put in your pocket. The $4,750.

Your Home

Next item on the list is your home. Even though you have a mortgage on it, your home could still be one of your biggest assets.

I lived in Washington, DC at a point in time where people could buy a home and have it double in value within a year or two.

(Of course, people later saw those property values do the exact opposite, too…Home ownership is not always the be all end all.)

Okay. Back to the point. How do you value your home?

This is what I did. I looked at Zillow or another site like that and saw what it estimated as my property value. And then I did a gut check. Because most of those sites use recent sales to calculate their estimates.

At one point in time I had a rental property in Colorado that was an older ranch-style home in a mature neighborhood with few sales in the immediate area. And I had a brand new two-bedroom condo in DC in a building where almost everyone had been locked into owning the home for the first two years.

Every time I looked at the property value for the house, I thought Zillow had it priced too high. There was no way anyone would pay over $200,000 for that house at that time.

No way. And at one point Zillow listed it as high as $215,000.

So I'd take Zillow's estimate and adjust it downward to something like $190,000. That was the value I used in my personal calculations.

I thought the exact opposite with the condo. I thought Zillow priced it too low because, again, there weren't good comparable sales available. It was in a good area and new but no one was allowed to sell their unit yet. On that one, I just kept Zillow's price.

(I like to be conservative in my estimates. So rather than bump up their number, I just stayed with the lower of the two options.)

Now, selling a home has costs. You will not get the value on Zillow even if it's 100% accurate. You generally have to pay a realtor a fee for the sale. An amount as high as six percent. Which means the liquidated value for your home is less than the value you list for it.

For liquidated value, I put the price from the value column minus six percent.

Let's do an example.

Let's say Zillow says your house is worth $300,000, but you're not so sure, so you list its value as $280,000.

You'd then list a liquidated value of $263,200.

(That's not actually what you get to take home unless your house is paid for, of course. Later when we calculate what you owe, we'll offset that amount with your outstanding mortgage balance.)

Your Car

Similar to the house situation. You can look up your car's value on the Kelley Blue Book website. Put in the type of car, mileage, condition, and it'll give you an estimated value.

But you have to be realistic about this, too.

A few years back they said my car was worth something like $8,000 if I sold to a dealer. I walked into a couple of dealers and one offered me $4,000 while the other offered me $6,000.

So realize that if you are selling off a car for money (as opposed to as a trade-in), that you may not receive the full value.

I'd probably take the blue book value and cut it down by 25% or so to be safe.

Actually, with my car, because it's not a high-value asset, I just list it with my other things at a value of about $3,000. Having gone through that experience, I'm now ultra conservative with the value I assign my vehicle.

Retirement Account At Your Employer

If you're with an employer who offers a 401(k), chances are you get a quarterly statement listing the value of your investments in the account.

But as long as you're with that employer, that money isn't really available to you.

You can usually borrow against it. Many plans allow plan participants, as you're called, to take an interest-free loan out against the balance of their account.

But you can't actually withdraw those funds until you leave.

(And then you have other issues to deal with.)

So if you have a 401(k) at your current employer, list the balance of the accounts as your value and then list the liquidated value as zero.

Yep, zero.

I know, you can take a loan against it. But that's not really an asset for you. That's like a line of credit.

It's like knowing your mom will loan you $5,000 if you're really desperate.

We don't want that in your list of liquidated assets.

So zero it out.

Same with any pension or profit sharing you have with your current employer.

(Note that this is why budgeting is an art as much as a science. My approach to it is this: If I get in serious trouble tomorrow, what can I do? What about if I know that things are going to go to hell next month? Or in six months? What can I do? What do I have that I can use?)

Forget all the fancy terms and theories.

What can you get your hands on?

And when?

And the reason we zero this out is that, as long as you're at that employer, the money you pull from your retirement account is a loan, the amount you can pull is limited, and you're expected to pay it back.

(Now, I don't get into it here, but I also track "available credit." That's what lines of credit, credit cards, etc. that I have access to. I list how much I have access to, how much I've already used, and what the interest rate for each one is. So, if I were at an employer and had a 401(k) there, I'd list the amount I could borrow in this area instead. If you do that, look at your plan materials to see how much you can borrow. I believe it's normally limited to 50% of the account value and there may also be a dollar limit on it as well. And it really is like a loan because you'll have to make monthly payments to pay it back and it'll be due in full if you leave that employer.)

Retirement Account From A Former Employer or Traditional IRA

What about a retirement account from a former employer? This one you can give a value. But not the value you'd want to give it. Same with a traditional IRA.

There are some exceptions (that we're not going to get into right here), but, in general, if you want to access the funds you have in your retirement account before you are of retirement age, you will have to pay penalties to do so.

Last I checked, in the United States any non-exempt withdrawal would result in a 10% penalty. Plus they keep 20% of the funds to cover taxes. So, no matter what, you can assume that you'll only get 70% of the value in your account. (100%-30% for penalties and tax withholding.)

If you're in a higher tax bracket (and taking that withdrawal may bump you into a higher tax bracket because the distribution is treated like income), you'll get even less. Well, you'll get the money when you withdraw it but the next year when you file your taxes, you'll have to pay that 10% penalty plus whatever your tax rate is on what you withdrew.

Long story short, for 401(k) plans from a former employer or traditional IRAs, the liquidated value should be 70% of the value of the account and possibly even less than that. (I use 50% to be very conservative.)

Let's do an example:

You have a 401(k) from your former employer that's worth $100,000. You can list that in your value column.

But in your liquidated value column, you should list $70,000. (Or less.)

If you're of retirement age, you still have to pay taxes on any withdrawals, so you should adjust your value by your current tax rate. And remember that the bigger the withdrawal, the higher that tax rate will be.

Keep in mind, you should only do this if you haven't rolled that old plan into your current employer plan. If you have, it, too, has zero value.

Roth IRA

A Roth IRA works differently because you already paid taxes on that money before you deposited it into the IRA account, so there is a possibility of being able to withdraw at least some of the money without any sort of penalty or taxes. I'm not going to try to walk through the nuances here. If you have a Roth, look up the rules and haircut your value appropriately to get your liquidated value.

529 Plans

Usually the funds in these plans are reserved for educational expenses. If you want to use the funds for other purposes, then you have to pay a 10% penalty and taxes on the earnings as if they were income. So if you're going to list your 529 plan as a general asset, then haircut it by 10% plus your tax rate. As above, that means that the maximum liquidated value you should assign it is about 70% of its value.

(Note that I am greatly simplifying things here. If you're someone with 529 plans and investment accounts and the like and you're living close to the edge so that you might need to suck money out of the accounts, it might behoove you to get a financial advisor involved who can tell you what the actual numbers are for your particular situation.)

Brokerage or Investment Accounts

I keep using this term, haircut, and the brokerage industry is where I pulled it from.

That's because most brokerage firms (you know, the guys who sell you stocks and bonds) are required to haircut their own securities holdings. The federal rules for brokerage firms acknowledge that just because you have a stock or bond that doesn't mean that when you go to sell it you'll actually get the current market value for it.

For example:

Say you own 10,000 shares of ABC stock priced at $5 that has a paper value of $50,000.

Depending on the nature of ABC stock, you might not come even close to getting that value for the stock when you try to sell it in two weeks.

If no one else is trying to sell that stock that day, the price will plummet. If lots of people are selling that day, the price may stay fairly level. It's hard to know in advance although certain types of securities tend to behave the same.

There's a very complicated regulation that broker-dealers have to follow that sets forth various percentages they should use based upon the general movement and riskiness of a security.

In general, government securities are much lower risk than equity securities and their price is considered more stable. Within equities some are much riskier than others. And then there's the problem of having all your eggs in one basket and how that's an additional risk and...

Bottom line for what we're doing here:

If you have equity securities holdings, discount them by 15%.

So list the current value of the holdings in the value

column and then list the liquidated value as 85% of that amount. If you want to get really specific, add a little more of a deduction for the commission you'll have to pay your broker.

The key here is to understand that investments are not static. They don't have the same value day-to-day. Not even bonds or government securities.

So you can't just assume that a security will be worth what you paid for it. Or what it was worth last week.

(Now, technically, I should've had you haircut the value of your retirement accounts the same way because chances are your funds in those accounts are invested in some sort of security or other. If not, they should be. But I think that's taking things to too much of an extreme when the goal here is to just try to get a handle on how you're doing and to realize that not everything you own is worth what you think it is. If it's a really large amount, though, and the majority of your assets, then consider cutting it by an additional 15%.)

Valuables/Collections

What about your antique watch collection? Or your comic book collection?

Honestly, unless you know you own something very valuable or are a bona fide collector who knows what you're doing, don't even bother with this one. Just include these in a general "things" category where you throw the value of everything else you own.

If you are a collector, then think about this the same way you did everything above. What do the collectors' guides say it's worth? And now, realistically, if you had to call your contacts tomorrow and sell off your collection, what would you actually receive?

That's your value vs. your liquidated value.

Things

Sometimes people underestimate the value of what they own. My brother has a few fancy TVs I'm sure he could sell off for a few hundred bucks if he needed to.

Usually people tend to do the opposite and overestimate the value of what they own. Just because you paid $150 for a pair of tennies doesn't mean anyone else will pay you a penny for them now that you've worn them once.

I have a number on my budget spreadsheet for things which includes the value of my car and furniture and computers and jewelry. It's a pretty low number, considering, but it's enough of a number that I think it's worth listing.

If you don't have much, skip this entry.

Now add it all up. What is the total value of your assets? What is their liquidated value?

Okay, that's what you own.

Now, what do you owe?

WHAT DO YOU OWE?

In finance circles this is sometimes phrased as "what are your liabilities"?

It's great to own things, but…

Many people owe more money for the things they own than those things are worth. And that's one way you can get in trouble.

So it's important to determine what you owe.

The first step is to list all your debts.

We're going to focus first on balances for all your loans like mortgages, car loans, student loans, etc.

These are the debts that are hanging over your head, ready to crush you if you stop paying for them, but that you don't have to pay off immediately.

A mortgage can hang there for thirty years. Make the monthly payment and you're fine. Miss it too many times and you no longer have a house.

So. What do you include?

First, go to your assets list and for each item on there,

determine whether you have a corresponding debt. Generally, you should only have corresponding debts for your house and your car.

Next, do you have any credit cards?

Or student loans?

Or any personal loans other than those above?

Do you have a tax liability? (Rare unless you're self-employed or had to enter into an installment plan at some point.)

For every debt you identify, list the balance and the interest rate you're paying on the debt.

Just in case you're not familiar with interest rates, let's discuss them for a second.

Most people, other than maybe your mother, will not loan you money for free. They want something for handing you cash. (Which is what they are doing when they issue you a credit card or a mortgage. They are taking money out of their pocket and making it available for you to use.)

Usually they demand payment in the form of interest.

So someone loans you $10,000 and then they charge a certain percentage every year for that privilege. With credit cards it can be in the 20%+ range.

If someone loans you $10,000 and they charge you 20% interest, at the end of that one year—assuming you don't pay any part of the debt—you now owe $12,000. The $10,000 you originally borrowed and 20% of $10,000 or $2,000.

If you then don't pay that debt off for another year, now you owe $14,400.

This is why people say it's BAD to have credit card debt. Because if you don't pay it off, it just gets bigger and bigger and bigger.

It's also why you shouldn't defer student loan debt too long even if you can. The interest rate on student loan debt isn't generally that high, but defer any loan that charges interest and the balance will keep growing and growing and growing…(assuming we aren't talking about a subsidized student loan where the government pays the interest for you).

Not fun.

Why do we care right now what the interest rates are? Because if you really get a handle on your finances you're probably going to want to start paying off some of your debts. And you want to put that money to the best possible use, which will likely include paying off high interest rate loans first.

(It may not. We'll discuss it in the debt guide. Right now we just need to know where you are before we go getting all complicated.)

Payoff Amount

One more thing in terms of the amount owed. The number you're looking for is the payoff amount.

For example, you may log into your student loan account and it says that you owe $9,324.41. Problem is, that's not actually the full amount you owe because the balance is going up every single day due to interest. Look around a bit and you'll find a payoff amount which will be something like $9,368.72. That's the amount you want.

Lots of times it isn't that different from the first amount you see, but it's enough of a difference that you want to track it.

Penalties

Some loans come with prepayment penalties. Hopefully you don't have any of these. If you do it means you were in a situation where you were naïve or where you had no choice but to accept a bad deal. A prepayment penalty exists when you have to pay extra money in order to get rid of the debt now. Think about that.

You owe $20,000. You come into some money and want to pay it off because you're paying 30% interest on the loan and want to get away from that as soon as possible. But for the privilege of no longer having to pay an obscene amount of interest, you have to pay $5,000 on top of what you owe already.

It sucks.

Avoid loans with prepayment penalties unless there is absolutely no other choice. A loan like that is almost guaranteed to be a loan that is bad for you.

But if you have one, note somewhere what the prepayment penalty is and when it expires.

Once you have all your debts listed, add 'em up and see what the total is. In an ideal world, your assets will be greater than your debts. Meaning that if you had to, you could liquidate everything you own and pay off everything you owe.

Chances are if you're young, financed college with student loans that you're still paying off, or you've needed to use debt to stay afloat, that you owe more than you own.

That isn't necessarily bad. It doesn't mean you can't live a happy life. It just means you owe more than you currently have so you need that debt to be there.

Okay, so that was the last number. Now that you know what you earn, what you spend, what you own, and what you owe, we can figure out where you stand financially. That's what we'll cover in the next section.

JUDGING YOUR
FINANCIAL HEALTH

EARNINGS VERSUS EXPENSES

First things first, do you earn more than you have to pay to expenses?

I'm going to continue to work with a one-month time period for this, but use the time period that makes sense for you and your situation.

So, between all of your income sources (that you can count as reasonable and expected month-to-month), do you bring in more money each month than you have to pay out?

The ideal answer to this question is yes.

This means that on a short-term basis, you're covering your expenses. As long as you keep your job, your expenses don't increase, and you don't have any longer-term savings needs, you are going to be just fine.

If you're earning less than you're spending each month, that doesn't necessarily mean that you're in trouble. As a consultant my income was variable enough that I considered my monthly income to be zero for planning purposes. I was doing quite well for most of the time that I was a consultant, but my answer on a month-to-month basis would have been no to this question.

Another scenario where this answer can be no and someone can be just fine is when you're in school. If you're paid a quarterly stipend or finance your living expenses through student loans that are paid out at the beginning of the quarter, then you'll have no monthly earnings to offset your monthly expenses.

In both of the two scenarios I mentioned, what you do need is to have savings or cash in the bank to cover your expenses. And you need to have enough of it to cover your expenses until the next time you're going to receive money.

Which leads to our next measure of your financial health…

MONTHS OF EXPENSES COVERED

How many months of expenses can you cover with cash on hand?

Take the amount of cash you have (that's the balances in your bank account and savings account and any literal cash you have available) and divide the total by your monthly expenses.

What do you get?

Even if you're earning more than you're spending each month, you want this number to be greater than one.

Because if it's greater than one then you know at the beginning of each month that you already have enough money to cover your bills for the month. You won't be scrambling and waiting to get paid on the 15th to turn around and pay that bill that was due on the 14th.

Ideally, you want this number to be at least three.

If it's three, then even if you didn't have any more money coming in the door you'd still be able to cover expenses for three months which would be enough to let you get a new job, sell something of value, cut back on your expenses, or borrow money.

If you're self-employed or have unreliable sources of income, you may want this number to be even higher. Say six or more. That lets you keep at what you're doing even when there's no immediate source of income coming in without panicking about how you're going to put food on the table.

As someone who is self-employed and has variable income month-to-month, I try to keep this number above six at all times but only panic when it falls below three. Where you set your panic point will depend on your own unique circumstances.

Another thing to consider is that the more you earn at your current job, the harder it will be to find a new one at that same level. If you lose a job flipping burgers at McDonald's that income is much easier to replace than if you lose a job as a CEO of a large company. The amount you keep in reserve should take that into consideration.

(Of course, the CEO is also likely to get some sort of severance package that will pay for a few months of expenses.)

Only you know how stable your job is and how likely you are to be able to find something to replace it. But always plan for worse than you think is possible. Add a couple months for that job search and assume your company could in fact fire you.

Okay. On to the next measure.

SHORT-TERM LIQUID NET WORTH

Is your short-term liquid net worth a positive number?

Your short-term liquid net worth takes your short-term assets and lines them up against your short-term liabilities. For short-term, I generally look at the next three months.

What cash can you get your hands on in the next three months? That's your bank account, your savings account, maybe a CD if you have one coming due soon, and any income you've earned but not yet been paid (that you can reasonably expect to be paid).

Don't include investment accounts in this number. Sure, you're very likely able to liquidate your stock holdings in the next three months, but you aren't planning on it. (If you need that money in the next three months it should not be invested in stocks. It should be in cash, a cash-equivalent, a CD, or a very low-risk bond fund or something like that.)

Also don't include things like your house in this number unless it's currently under contract and you've already passed inspection.

This is money you, in the routine process of living your life, expect to have in the next three months.

This isn't a measure of what you can scrounge up if you get desperate. It's what you expect to have in hand in the near future.

Now, look at your short-term liabilities. What debt are you carrying that is coming due in the next three months? (I don't actually include monthly expenses in this figure. This is more looking at the fact that my quarterly estimated tax payment is due next month and I owe the IRS $X for it. You can, though.)

This may be buying out your car lease. Or a downpayment on that house you're about to buy. For me, it includes my credit card balance because I do aim to pay that off every month.

The goal here is to make sure that you have cash free and available to pay the debts that you need to pay in the short-term.

Because, as it turns out, you can carry as much debt as people will give you and be fine as long as you're able to pay those debt payments when they come due. So, are you fine?

(By the way, that's not always the smartest thing to do, because life does change on a whim and not always for the best and finding yourself behind on hundreds of thousands of dollars in debt payments is never fun. But you *can* do it, technically.)

The key to not falling behind is to make sure that you always have enough money to pay what you owe when you owe it.

Think about that for a minute.

If you always have enough cash to pay your bills, then you'll never have late payment fees. Or trigger punitive interest rates. Or bounce checks. Or get evicted.

As long as you stay ahead of your payments, you're fine.

You might be stressed as hell and hate the job you feel you have to keep in order to pay those debts, but you'll be okay.

The reason you want to look at this measure is because money does you no good if it's in the wrong place. If you need to pay your bills this month and the only assets you have are long-term assets, you're in trouble. A million dollars in your 401(k) does you no good when you have no cash in the bank to pay next month's bills.

It's like knowing there's a brand new roll of toilet paper on the kitchen counter when you're in the back bathroom and need it. Great that you have it, but if it's not where you need it when you need it it's no use to you.

So take the liquidated value of your short-term assets and subtract the value of your short-term liabilities.

You need this number to be a positive number. Otherwise you're not going to be able to pay your bills.

If it isn't positive, figure out why. Is that going to get you into trouble? Are you facing a situation where you're going to owe money next month and have no way to pay it?

If so, you need to take steps now to keep that from happening.

Better to have this number be positive and have issues with long-term debts that far outweigh your long-term assets than to have this number be a negative number.

(I know people really like to pay off their student loans early. And, trust me, I get it. Twenty years of paying for student loans every month sucks. But if you pay off your student loans—a long-term liability and take away your cash on hand so you can't pay next month's bills, then that's a poor decision. Always make sure you have the NOW covered before you worry about tomorrow.)

If you don't want to go into the debt death spiral, find a way to pay your bills every month. Sell plasma if you have to. But pay your bills on time.

And keep in mind that just because this number is positive doesn't mean you have your financial house in order. But it does mean you can get through the next few months okay and that's important.

Next, let's talk about where you could still be falling short.

LONG-TERM GOALS

Are you saving for your long-term goals?

I don't know what your long-term goals are. It could be that you want to save money for retirement. Or buy a house. Or pay for your kids' college education. (Although I put myself through college just fine and I'm pretty sure your kids can do so, too, and may even be better off if they have to because it'll teach them to value that education and time spent at college.)

Maybe you want a new car. Or to take a big vacation.

So, are you saving money towards that goal?

If you're worried about retirement, are you contributing to your company's retirement plan? Or funding your own personal retirement account?

If so, are you putting away enough money? Not sure? Run one of those retirement calculators and see.

(And if you have a company match—where they put in just as much money as you do up to a certain percent—and you're paying your bills just fine and you've already met your short-term savings needs by having a bit of a reserve in the bank, then please, oh, please, contribute to the account at least up to the match amount. That's like getting a 100% return on your investment immediately.)

Same question for any of those other goals:

Are you putting money away?

Is it enough to let you achieve your goal when you want to achieve it?

Okay. So let's say you earn more than you spend each month, you have a few months in reserve, you're saving for everything you should be and are on track to achieve all your goals, what next?

SUSTAINABILITY

Is the life you're living sustainable?

Things can look great on paper and you can be months away from disaster.

How?

A few ways.

One, you can be in the type of career that flies high and then crashes and burns. Many people who were involved in the mortgage industry when it was hot can probably tell you about earning six-figures for a few years and having new mortgages to underwrite every time they turned around or closing on a new home sale every few days.

If they stayed with it long enough they can also tell you about how sales dried up. Interest rates skyrocketed and no one was buying anymore. No refinances, no new home sales. Nothing.

Same thing happens in the financial services industry. Some young thing gets hired into the investment banking division and thinks they're going to make millions forever.

Three years later they can't find a job that'll pay them $60,000 a year.

Two, you can be getting by day-to-day just fine, but have made some poor financial choices that are going to bite you in the butt tomorrow. Like doing an interest-only loan in a down market. Or having an adjustable rate mortgage when interest rates are on the rise. Or taking out no interest loans against your credit card that you can't pay off before the promotional period so you're going to end up with 23% interest rates on debt you can't get rid of next year.

Sure, yeah, as long as you can pay off your short-term liabilities with your short-term assets, you're fine.

But if you know that one side of that equation is shaky—that your income or assets are going to tank or that your liabilities are about to skyrocket—you're headed for a cliff and a fiery crash at the bottom of it.

Also, consider that maybe your shaky foundation isn't obvious.

Ask yourself: Am I the type of employee that's the last one to get fired? Or will I be one of the first? Do you show up every day and work your fingers to the bone? Or do you do the least amount you have to? Do you get along with your co-workers or, at least, your bosses? Or do you rub everyone the wrong way?

It can seem like the job you have now will last forever, but that's not necessarily the case. And not always in your control. If the market tanks and your company has to cut costs by firing people, will you be on the chopping block?

What about if you do spot work. Ask yourself: How steady is it? Do you get repeat customers? Or does it seem like you're constantly starting over from scratch each day?

Only you can judge your situation. But look at it realistically. If someone tells you that all the fundamentals have changed—that this time will be different than the last time—don't believe them. If you're in an industry that's known to work in cycles, expect and plan for them.

Next. Another question that's close on the heels of this one.

LONG-TERM CAREER PROSPECTS

What are your long-term prospects of continuing like this?

Some careers are more sustainable than others. If you're an accountant, you'll be able to do that job from twenty-five to sixty-five. But a pro football player? His career is pretty much maxed out before forty. Sometimes long before forty.

That goes for jobs like construction and waitressing, too. No one's going to fire you when you get to fifty, but standing on your feet for those long hours or trying to physically do the job is going to wear on you to the point that you may not be able to sustain it for that long.

So look at what you're doing and ask yourself how much longer you can do this for.

I know some folks in finance who are in very high stress positions. It's not a matter of physical stress, although they do seem to drop dead of heart attacks a lot, but of mental exhaustion.

Is what you're doing today sustainable for the long-term? If you're working hundred hour weeks and keeping everything going, can you keep working those hundred-hour weeks forever? If not, for how long?

In the same way, if you have seasonal or variable income or do spot work, how long can you continue to do so successfully?

This came up with my consulting work. I earned really good money on projects, but most of my contracts came from one individual. If that individual left their employer, which they did after I left, what were the odds of my finding someone else to send me work?

And what about expenses. How sustainable is it to work in the area you're working earning what you're earning? Many metropolitan areas go through cycles where costs go through the roof, but wages don't. Can you handle that situation?

A few more measures to consider:

VARIABILITY OF EXPENSES

How variable are your expenses?

Ideally, you will spend about the same amount every month.

If that's not the case, you are going to have a much harder time managing your finances.

The most insidious of these are discretionary expenses. This is your shopping habit. Or your bar tab. Or your penchant for going gambling. Or for taking trips.

This is when you blow your budget out of the water with unplanned purchases. It can just be a matter of going to the grocery store and picking up a bunch of crap you don't need and spending an extra $75 for the week.

If you're struggling to get your finances under control, you need to tame your expenses.

Look at the last six months and see how much your expenses varied month to month. Compare that to your monthly income. If the variance between your highest expense month and your lowest expense month was more than 10% of your monthly income, consider that a red flag.

You may be doing just fine at paying your bills even if it is more than 10%, but you're likely out of control with your spending and if your income changes you'll very quickly find yourself in trouble.

And, next:

AVAILABLE CREDIT

What credit do you have available to you and how expensive is it?

Sometimes life takes a nasty turn. If you needed to, what could you borrow tomorrow?

Look to your credit cards, the overdraft line on your bank accounts, any lines of credit you have at the bank, the borrowable balance on your company retirement account.

(If you don't have an overdraft line of credit at your bank, apply for one now. Basically, if something does go wrong and you're about to bounce a check, the bank will pull money in from that line of credit to cover it so you don't get hit with bounced check fees or overdraft fees. Very, very valuable to have in place even if you never use it. Worth $10 a year or whatever they charge for it.)

I keep a list of total credit available, amount already borrowed, remaining amount available, and the interest rate that each one currently charges. Make sure that you have enough credit available that you can cover an emergency expense like a new transmission for your car. Or your rent payment.

You don't want to draw on your lines of credit. This is not "how much of a shopping spree can I go on." It's "do I have some fallback sources of funds in case the worst happens."

Say you lose your job. Hopefully you have three months of expenses in the bank. And when you run out of that? Hopefully you have another three months of expenses available on your lines of credit. That gives you six months to work things out and get back on track.

You'll be three months of expenses in debt, but you'll have at least managed to pay your bills while you were out of work.

The more credit available, the better in my opinion. (Assuming you can control your use of it. If you immediately spend any credit someone gives you then don't have any credit because it's just more debt hanging over your head. Credit is a bit like alcohol. If you can't handle it, then don't touch it.)

You want as much credit as possible because you never know when a bank or credit card will decide to cut back on your available credit. I had one card I rarely used that was finally cut from $7,500 to $500. Good thing it wasn't my only source of credit when that happened.

Do try to arrange credit from more than one source. For example, open a line of credit with your bank and then open a credit card with a different bank. Or have two types of credit cards, Visa and Amex, for example, issued by different banks.

It's always a good idea to make sure you aren't completely dependent on one source of credit.

Okay. One final measure before we wrap this up:

LATE PAYMENTS AND BOUNCED CHECKS

It's actually possible to have all of the above looking great and still be terrible at managing your finances. Maybe you earn a lot of money, don't spend as much as you earn, are in a good stable job in a good area, are saving for all your goals, and have lots of available credit for an emergency.

That doesn't mean you have your act together.

If you're bouncing checks or failing to pay your bills on time, you're ruining your credit. Maybe that doesn't matter to you if you're earning enough money to cover your expenses, but credit can be that safety net that keeps you from going into freefall if your circumstances change. And most of us need credit at some point. To buy a house. Or a car. To get a new job.

Good credit is invaluable.

Not to mention that bouncing checks or missing payments is just throwing your money away. There are fees associated with this. You bounce a check, your bank charges you money, and sometimes so does the person you wrote the check to. You make a late payment on your credit card and suddenly you're paying 27% interest on your balance.

If you're in this situation you have to have to have to get things under control. This is priority one. Pay your bills and pay them on time.

ADDITIONAL THOUGHTS

Managing your finances is as much art as science. And what's necessary for each person will be different.

The key is to be able to pay your monthly expenses without stress and anxiety and to be able to save for whatever long-term goals you have whether that's home ownership or a trip around the world.

The measures discussed are just some ways of tracking your financial health. Where you set your own limits will vary based upon your comfort level with risk and your own individual circumstances.

The first step is to make sure you're paying your bills every month and paying them on time.

And remember, you can think you're doing just fine because you *are* paying your bills every month, but you're not because you aren't going to meet your longer-term goals. Or you're just one illness, one lost job, or one unexpected expense from disaster.

If you can, always have a cushion. Always have a fallback plan. Know where you're going if this doesn't work. And where you're going after that. And where you're going after that.

Okay. Now that you've seen how "healthy" you are financially, let's look at some strategies for improving your finances.

STRATEGIES FOR IMPROVING

STRATEGIES FOR IMPROVING
INITIAL THOUGHTS

Now it's time to talk about strategies for improving your financial health. Some are basic tricks to fool you into saving more or spending less and some require a complete overhaul of your life. What works for you will depend very much on your unique situation and needs, so take what works and ignore the rest.

(Although, if you find that you're still not getting to where you need to be, you might want to circle back and see if you should try one of the tips you skipped the first time around.)

So, without further ado, let's get started with the first trick.

OVERESTIMATE EXPENSES
UNDERESTIMATE INCOME

This trick helped me so much when I was in college. It's harder to pull off now when you can access your bank account balance online 24/7. But when I was in school I had to either call into the 800 number to hear the list of my most recent transactions or I had to wait for the monthly statement to arrive. Which meant that between those times, I relied on my check register to know what money I had available.

And because I didn't feel any pressing need to balance my checkbook down to the last penny, I would round everything.

If I deposited a check for $537.22 into my account, I just recorded it as $535.

If I wrote a check for $122.31 for my utilities, I recorded it as $125.

Note that I always rounded expenses up and always rounded income down.

Now, let's look at that in a little more detail to see what it does.

The real numbers are this: I earned $537.22 and paid out $122.31, leaving me with a balance of $414.91.

With my approach: I earned $535 and paid out $125 leaving me with a balance of $410.

Right there in two transactions I ended up with $4.91 that I didn't realize I still had. My check ledger would read $410 and that's what I'd assume was available for me to spend.

Which was great for me. Because I was living close enough to the edge that right towards the end of the month I needed a little extra. That's when I'd go through and find out what my actual bank account balance was and find that I had $45 more than I thought, which would pay for groceries for the week.

It's just a little mental trick that gives you a cushion. And it won't work at all if you tell yourself that you obviously have more money than you think you do so spend that extra money without checking how much you actually have.

If you can't use it with your bank account, you can still use it for budgeting.

For example, I list all of my expenses as slightly higher than they are. I round up to the nearest five dollars. So that phone bill that's $83.21 becomes $85. And that insurance bill that's $72.51 becomes $75.

I do the exact opposite with my income. If I'm supposed to earn $532.21, I'll either list that as $530 or, if I have the wiggle room to do so, $500.

The key to this is to always overestimate your expenses—make them higher than they really are—and underestimate your income—make it lower than it really is. That way the math is always working in your favor.

So $72.21 becomes $75 if it's a bill and $70 if it's income no matter what the rounding rules say to do with that number.

This isn't about accuracy. It's about building a cushion into your budget.

And, of course, I'm assuming here that you keep a monthly budget. (If you don't, you should. All those numbers we talked about in the *Earn Spend Own Owe* guide? You should track them all on an ongoing basis and update them at least twice a month if not more often. I tend to update them every time I pay a large bill or when I'm paid.)

Okay, so that's just one little trick I use. It may work for you, it may not.

What else?

EVEN OUT YOUR EXPENSES

I mentioned this in the prior guides, but some bills, like your utilities, will vary month-to-month. Utilities are charged based on usage, so that coldest month of the year will likely cost you more than a nice spring month with mild weather. This makes it challenging to budget month-to-month since there's such variation in the amount you're billed.

Many utility companies offer billing programs where they charge you a set amount per month. It's higher than you'd pay in the low months, but less than you'd pay in the high months. The key here, though, is it's consistent month-to-month. You know what you're going to have to pay every single month. No ugly surprises that leave you scrambling to make up the difference between what you thought you'd owe and what you actually owe. And no need to save in the low months to be able to pay for the high months.

If you haven't already, I'd recommend signing up for a program like this.

If you can't sign up for a program like this you could create your own version. If you're living in the same place and plan to be for a while, come up with your own estimate of your average cost and start paying that amount in the low months even when the bill is for a lesser amount.

How would this work?

Say you decide that $125 is the average amount you pay per month over the course of a year. When spring rolls around and your bill is only $75, pay $125. The next month when your bill is only $80, pay $125. The month after that when the bill is $90, pay $125. The month after that when the bill is $150, you still write a check for $125. And the month after that when it's $225, you can still write a check for $125 because you're covered for the increases in cost based upon what you paid in those first three months.

Over those five months you paid in a total of $625 by paying $125 a month. And you were charged a total of $620. You still have a $5 credit.

Now, this depends on you believing you'll have an ongoing relationship with the company in question and knowing that they'll properly credit your overpayment. And you'll have to keep forcing yourself to write that $125 check every month even when your bill shows a credit and says you don't have to pay anything at all like in month three of the scenario above.

But it can be a nice way to even out that expense. And obviously, you have to pay the minimum amount due. So if you don't get it right and one month you in fact owe $175, you have to pay that $175 that month.

Most of your monthly bills will be predictable and consistent. The place where most of us run into issues is discretionary spending. Like going to the bar. Or that daily coffee habit.

So how do you even that one out?

You could use gift cards for anything that isn't an essential purchase. At the beginning of the month, buy yourself a gift card in the amount that you're allowed to spend at Starbucks for that month. Use it until it's gone and then that's it for that month. No more Starbucks.

Or set aside a certain amount of cash you're allowed to spend and only have that cash with you when you go out. So $40 at the bar and only take the cash and no credit card with you. (Me, I'm a little too nervous that something bad would happen and I'd need that credit card to actually pull this one off, but I can see it working.)

The key here is that you want to know, as much as you possibly can, how much you need to earn in a given month. And the only way to know that is to keep your expenses under control and consistent.

So consider subscription services or memberships instead of one-off purchases. I can think of at least three subscription book services, for example. (Of course, if you don't use them, these are a good place to then cut costs if you need to tighten your belt a bit.)

One final suggestion for evening out your expenses: If you currently pay your insurance on a bi-annual or quarterly basis, look at changing that into a monthly payment. It might cost a little more, but if you're struggling to make that payment when it comes due each time, it'll help you manage things better because, again, it'll be steady and consistent month-to-month.

Which leads to the next recommendation.

MAKE YOUR INCOME CONSISTENT

For some people, this isn't an issue. If you have a salaried job, you've already done this. But there are a number of people out there who live by picking up odd jobs here or there. Or who have hourly jobs with inconsistent hours. Or who work in a job with a sales-based pay structure where you never know month-to-month or week-to-week what you'll earn.

Get away from that as much as you can.

As an example, my brother is a salesman. When he first started his career he worked for a company that paid him almost entirely in commissions. Now, my brother could sell snow to Eskimos and they'd thank him for introducing him to this amazing new product, so the issue was never whether my brother could make sales.

The issue was two-fold. One, could the company he worked for pay him his commissions when they were due? And, two, would the customers he sold the product to pay on time? Because in that type of job you're generally only paid when the customer pays.

Sometimes the answer to both of those questions was yes and my brother did just fine. He sold enough, so as long as everyone was paying on time, he was golden.

But then clients stopped paying on time. And his boss stopped paying him even when customers did pay on time. And that meant that my brother had no idea what he would earn, if anything, on payday. It made it very, very challenging to pay his bills on time.

Fortunately, he eventually moved to a new company. Same field. Same clients. But this company guaranteed him a monthly salary. Sure, if he falls too low in his sales numbers they'll fire him, but that's not a big concern for my brother. What was a big concern was knowing what he was going to earn every two weeks.

(This company also pays him an annual bonus if he exceeds his sales quotas, so he still has the upside that a good salesman wants.)

By moving from the first company, where each paycheck was an unknown quantity, to the second company, where each paycheck is the same amount every single month, he managed to do what he's good at while keeping his income steady.

So look at how you earn your money and see if there's a way to make it more consistent.

Let's take a weird example.

Say you make money by going around the neighborhood, seeing that someone's yard needs mowing, and knocking on their door with an offer to mow their yard. It's good money when you can find enough yards that need mowing, but some weeks you can't find anyone in need of help.

Here's what you do: The next time you find someone whose yard needs mowing and they agree to let you do the work, you do a good job and, when it comes time to pay you, you offer to come back in two weeks and do it again. Not everyone will say yes, but those that do are now customers of yours. You show up every two weeks and do a good job and they will pay you to do that work every two weeks.

You now have some consistency and income to count on. Much better than wandering around hoping that someone will throw some work your way.

Whatever it takes, make your income as consistent as you can. That may even require changing jobs like my brother did which can be scary as hell. But if you don't know what you're earning and when, you're much more likely to end up in financial troubles.

A good way to cushion that?

HAVE ONE MONTH OF EXPENSES TO START THE MONTH

A good way to deal with variable income or to just make sure you will pay all your bills on time is to keep at least one month's worth of expenses in your account at all times. That way you hit the first of the month and you already know that you're going to be able to pay your bills for the month. This lets you focus your energy on making enough money for the next month.

For some this may be really easy to do. Just don't spend all of that annual bonus or tax refund. Hold onto enough to equal one month of expenses.

Or work an extra job to build up that reserve.

For others, it may require taking one step back first like I did many years ago.

WARNING: This trick is not for everyone. If you know that you are bad with your credit cards or lines of credit, do not do this.

This is something I did right after I graduated college and it really did help me out. So I'm going to share it with you with the understanding that this is not for everyone.

It's only for someone who can do this once and then never have to do it again. And to pull that off you need to be earning enough to cover your expenses each month.

If you are, and you can't just hold back some money to get that cushion, consider taking money from a line of credit or credit card to make this happen.

Yes, you will be increasing your overall debt. Not something most people would recommend.

But if doing so means you never bounce another check or miss another payment deadline, it may well be worth it.

Think about how much less stressed you'll be if you don't have to cross your fingers and pray that the check you mailed on the 13th won't be cashed until after your paycheck hits on the 15th.

You'll know you're covered every month.

And that may well be worth that extra $25 a month in payments and interest you pay to take that money from your line of credit.

Like I said, do not do this if you don't have the discipline to use that money to pay your bills. You have to be able to let money sit in your account for a month without spending it or this won't work. Because once you establish this cushion then each paycheck is on hold to pay the next month's bills.

You cannot look at your bank account and think, "Ooh, I have a $1,000 in there. I can buy this Xbox." No, no, no. You must have the discipline to not spend that money or all this will do for you is put you more in debt.

If you try it once and fail, do not try it again. But if you can manage it, it might just save you from a lot of stress and heartache.

So what do you do if you're currently spending more than you earn each month? Or if you're not able to meet your long-term goals with what you earn?

Well, the obvious:

EARN MORE

How?

If you want to stay at your current job, you can apply for a promotion, ask for extra hours, or ask for a raise.

Now, to get any of the above you need to be the type of employee that your company wants to promote, give a raise, or give extra hours. Which may mean busting your butt for a while to prove yourself.

(As a former manager, I can assure you that "I want to earn more" or "I need to earn more" wasn't a very persuasive argument to me, because everyone wanted to earn more. But my best employee asking for more? That person I wanted to keep and was willing to do what I could to keep them.)

If you want to be a good employee, you will need to prioritize work over other considerations. If you ask your boss for more hours and he calls you up and says he has a project that needs to be done immediately, you say yes. That may mean cancelling that weekend trip. Or not attending your kid's soccer game. Or not going to kickball this week. But you make that sacrifice to show your boss that giving this opportunity to you was the right choice.

What you do not under any circumstances do is ask for more hours and then say you can't take them on when you're given the opportunity. Guess who won't get called next time there's a last-minute project with extra hours? You.

And you need to do well at your job. Half-assing it will not work. You need to be the superstar if you want to make more money at your current job.

Another option if the current job doesn't offer possibilities is to pick up additional work on the side. Most people work a forty-hour workweek. Well, there are 168 hours in a week. Take out ten hours a day for sleep and eating and commuting and forty hours for the job you already have and you have 58 hours available to take on another job.

I had a summer where I worked one job during the day, volunteered two days a week, and worked sixty hours a week at a night and weekend job. And I still had time to sleep and occasionally hang out with friends. It wasn't fun and I didn't want to do it forever, but it can be done.

Put in the hours you need to to make the money you need, even if that means you don't get to enjoy all the fun things in life right now.

You don't do it forever, hopefully, but you do it if that's the only choice available at the time.

Your third option is to leave your current job and find something better. When I was in college I was forced to do this and realized that I'd been a fool for not doing so sooner. I had shown up the first week of school and taken the first retail job I found. I didn't look around, I didn't see if I could earn more somewhere else. It paid money and I needed money. Well, when I lost that job, I found out I could work at a temp agency with benefits for almost twice what I'd been paid at the retail job.

The whole time I was working forty hour weeks at that retail job I could've been working twenty hour weeks at that temp job and earning the same amount of money.

So if you're not making enough to cover your expenses, look around. See what else is out there.

I ran into this again in my professional career. I thought I was paid well at my job and had no interest in leaving. But I had an opportunity to talk to another company and they made me a job offer that was 25% higher than my current salary. (And, it turns out, was low for that position at that company.) When I told my company, do you know what they did? They matched the offer.

Think about that. They were willing to pay me 25% more per year than I was earning, but I never knew it because I never bothered to see what else was out there.

So if you're good at what you do, look around. See what's out there.

(And, even though this is a guide about budgeting realize that you'll have more income opportunities the more dedicated and hard-working you are at your job. Whatever that job is. Those opportunities may not even come from your current employer. They may come from a client or a friend who sees how hard you work.)

Now let's talk about the other side of that coin. You can earn more or...

SPEND LESS

If you're not meeting all your financial goals and making more money isn't possible, then spend less.

I have things I love. Coca-Cola, my cellphone, internet, cable.

But if I were in financial trouble? None of those things are *necessary*. Convenient, yes. Necessary? No.

Even though I work from home and need internet access to publish what I write, there are other options.

Pretty much everywhere on the planet seems to have free wi-fi these days. And if they don't, the local library does. And it provides computers if you need those.

And as handy as my cellphone is, I don't need a fancy one if things get bad. I can go get one of those pay-as-you-go plans for $15 a month and try not to use my phone as much as possible.

It's hard to cut back on things you're used to. That afternoon coffee run. That $12 lunch you grab each day. HBO. Your monthly cut and color.

But think about how much you can spend on little things like that that you don't really need.

Let's say you spend $15 a day on coffee and lunch. That's $300 a month.

Nobody wants to, but wouldn't it be better to drink the coffee from the break room and bring a bag lunch and save $300 towards your retirement so you don't have to show up at that crap job for the rest of your life?

It's not easy, believe me.

I had to cut back to the bone at one point. I was working a sales job that paid just enough to cover my rent and leave me about $20 a week for groceries. No phone. No internet. No going out with friends. No Coca-Cola (which was a HUGE loss for me back then.)

I managed.

I made large batches of soup once a week using potatoes, carrots, and cheap meat. I had dinner at relatives' houses three times a week and asked for leftovers. And I had no luxuries, not even a phone.

It's doable. Not easy, but doable. And there's nothing like living that way to motivate you to find a different solution.

So, if you're in this situation look at what you spend money on and ask yourself what you actually need to keep a roof over your head and food in your belly. Everything else is optional. Get rid of it if you can.

And if cutting back to the bone isn't enough, then you have to find a way to make more or to reduce those costs you can't avoid, like rent.

Which leads us to the next possible step:

MOVE SOMEWHERE CHEAPER

This is one of the hardest things to consider. But if you're barely surviving where you are, consider moving.

I'll give you an example. When I graduated college, I moved to Denver, Colorado. A friend of mine moved to New York City. We both found jobs and worked at entry-level positions. Three years later we were both at the same companies as when we'd started and had both done well at our jobs.

I was able to buy a three-bedroom, two-bath home with a nice little yard. My friend, whose rent was almost double my mortgage payment, lived a full hour from work in a tiny studio where she could touch both walls by stretching out her hands.

Why the difference?

Because some areas of the country are simply more expensive to live in than others. Denver is just now hitting a point where it's going to be more expensive to live in, but there are still many, many cities where you can live well on a low amount of money.

It can be hard to move away from family, friends, and community. And for some people it's not even something to consider.

But if you aren't firmly embedded in your community, then consider moving somewhere cheaper. You may take a short-term hit, but in the long-run moving somewhere cheaper may be the single-most important financial decision you make.

If you do move, look for somewhere with a low cost of living AND a low unemployment rate. And, ideally, a place with the types of work you're qualified to do.

And don't be afraid to be creative and look outside your country.

A few years back New Zealand was dying for construction workers to come and help rebuild after the massive Christchurch earthquakes. I'm pretty sure they were paying huge incentives and also paying to relocate people there. Be open to crazy opportunities like that. Most people won't take them, so if you're willing to, you could find a really, really good life.

Okay, so what other things can you do to manage your finances?

PAY BILLS WHEN RECEIVED
OR WHEN YOU GET PAID

Sure, that bill may not be due for two weeks. But if you know that you're the type of person to spend any money in your account then pay your bills as soon as you get paid so that money isn't there to tempt you.

With online bill pay you don't even have to wait for the statement to arrive. Just log into your account and pay the bill now. At least you know the funds are going towards what they need to.

AUTOMATE YOUR INVESTMENTS

If you want to save for long-term goals but never seem to manage it, arrange to automatically save that money before you ever even receive your paycheck.

Many companies have arrangements where you can put money into a savings account before you're paid. 401(k)s work like this. Your company takes that percentage you've designated towards your retirement right off the top and then sends you the rest. After a paycheck or two you don't even think about that money as yours.

Many banks have similar programs where you can sign up for an automatic funds transfer to move funds from your checking account into a separate savings account. Schedule the transfer for the day after you're paid and you won't even have to think about saving that money.

If you have a long term goal you're saving towards, see if you can automate that investment so you never even see the money before it's set aside. It removes the chance that you'll try to use the funds for some other purpose.

And if you get a pay raise? Up the contribution amount before the raise ever hits. You won't even notice the difference.

AUTOMATE YOUR PAYMENTS

If you're making enough money every month but you're still getting hit with late payment fees, then you probably have an issue with organization or focus. (Or stress. My friend fell apart when her marriage hit the rocks.)

To get around this, automate as many payments as you can. These days almost every single bill can be paid through automated payments. Even your credit card.

So if you feel comfortable that your income is steady and consistent enough, automate as much as you can. Money comes in, money goes out, the only thing you have to do is make sure to keep making enough money to cover the withdrawals.

Now, I don't automate my credit card payment because that's the one that varies the most and I like to look at it each month. But everything else I do automate if I can.

And for my credit card what I do is:

SIGN UP FOR ACCOUNT ALERTS

Most credit cards will alert you when they issue your statement. And when your payment is due. If you haven't already, sign up for these alerts. It's just a little extra nudge to make sure you're taking care of your business.

Me, I leave the e-mail in my inbox until I've gone in and scheduled the payment for the month. Reminds me I need to take care of that.

Other companies can alert you, too.

My phone alerts me when my minutes are about to run out so I can cut back on calls for the rest of the month.

Sign up for any alert you can from your bank, your credit card, or your other bills.

LOWER YOUR INTEREST RATES

If you've had a credit card for a long time and consistently pay your bills it's possible that you can get the credit card to lower the amount of interest it charges you. I was able to do this with one of my cards. I think the card had a 24.99% interest rate at the time and when I called the company they lowered the rate to 16.99%. Still not as great as getting rid of that debt, but at least more of the money I paid each month went to my balance instead of interest.

Let me just throw in a word of caution here about any sort of loan consolidation to get down your payments and "lower your interest rate." I used to get these ads all the time for my student loans, but if you read the fine print you'll find that the new "lower" rate is actually a blended rate based upon the rate you pay across all of your loans. Problem with doing this is that you can't then pay off your higher interest rate loan first because everything has been rolled into one much larger loan that incorporates that higher rate. So if you can do it, keep them separate so you can make extra payments to the higher interest one.

What you can do with student loans and some other long-term debt is arrange for automatic payments. Often this will lower your interest rate by a quarter of a percent or so. Not much, but every little bit counts.

ARRANGE FOR CREDIT
OR MORE CREDIT

First things first, if you can't control yourself when it comes to credit, then do not do this. Credit is like alcohol. If you can't manage yourself around it, don't touch it.

But for those who can.

If you don't have overdraft protection on your bank account, try to arrange for it. This should just be there for emergencies where something goes wrong and you don't have funds in the account to cover your bills, but it can be a lifesaver that keeps you from bouncing a check.

If you don't have a credit card, sign up for one. And use it a little here or there so you can build up a credit history. That will help you qualify if you later want to buy a car or house. It lets a potential lender see that you've been loaned money before and paid for it.

If no one will give you a credit card, you can do a pre-paid card. You give them $500. They give you the card. You use the card and pay the payments each month. Yes, you're borrowing your own money, but it's a way to rebuild or build credit if no one's willing to take a risk on you by lending you their money.

If you only have a few hundred dollars worth of credit available, try to get more. The more credit you have available (without using it, I might add), the better.

Again, only do this if you aren't going to turn around and max your credit out right away. This isn't about digging a deeper hole for yourself, but is instead about giving yourself more of a safety net.

Credit should be there as a back-up plan. When your car suddenly dies and you have no way to get to work, having that credit available will let you get the car fixed so you can keep earning money.

If you don't have a credit card or line of credit, then everything you do depends on the cash you have on hand. And most of us don't have that much on hand to sail through the emergencies that life always seems to throw at us.

CONVERT SHORT-TERM DEBT
TO LONG-TERM DEBT

The other nice thing about credit is that it lets you convert short-term debt into long-term debt. Depending on where you are financially, it may be much better to pay $500 a month for a year than $6,000 this month. That's what credit lets you do.

Your car breaks down? Use credit to transform that $2,000 mechanic's bill into a long-term debt that you pay on a monthly basis.

Now, be careful here. Only do this for items of value or essential needs. Because you're going to pay more over the long term for whatever it is. But sometimes doing this can be the difference between financial ruin and financial success.

Think about a medical bill. Say you have to have your appendix removed. And insurance covers some of it, but you now owe $20,000 for what insurance didn't cover.

No way you can pay that, right? So you can ignore the bill and say you can't pay it and stop answering your phone so the collectors can't harass you and wait for the hospital to write it off and report it on your credit report which will make all other credit you apply for cost more.

OR you can call up the hospital, explain that you don't have $20,000 to pay that bill, but could pay $100 a month towards it, and keep your credit clean.

Before you ever give up on paying for something, try to call the company first and see what you can make happen. Sometimes there's nothing to be done. But a lot of times a company would rather you paid them a little bit at a time than never paid them.

Of course, the best approach, if you can, is to pay that bill now. But if you can't…then try to work out a different solution.

And keep in mind I am not recommending that you use this approach to buy that fancy TV through the local rent-to-own place. (Avoid, avoid, avoid.) That leads to the final piece of advice:

LET GO OF IMPRESSING OTHERS

This may be the single-most important thing that you can do for your finances and mental well-being. Many of us feel compelled to own pretty things or nice clothes or spend thousands on our appearance each year not because we want to but because we're worried about impressing everyone else. Or keeping up with them.

Who wants to be the only person on the block who isn't driving a new car?

You do.

Because if you can ignore what everyone is doing and stop caring about what they think of you, then you can stop buying all that ridiculous shit you don't need and get your finances in order and save for what really matters.

I will tell you, the trips I've taken to Iceland and Guatemala and New Zealand and Thailand are far more valuable than the one or two compliments I received on some new outfit I bought ten years ago.

Really sit down and figure out what matters to you. And realize that most people out there are not worth impressing. Not in the slightest.

Don't let trying to keep up or trying to show them that you "belong" bankrupt you.

If you have the funds to meet all your goals and buy all the fancy clothes and gadgets, then fine. Enjoy. But most of us don't, so you have to choose.

Do you want to be stress-free and able to own a home and take trips and retire at a reasonable age? Or do you want to impress Joe Nobody down the street?

CONCLUSION

So that's it. That's how you start down the path to reaching your financial goals. You figure out where you are now—what you earn, what you spend, what you own, what you owe—and then you figure out where you're weak and need to improve things to make your goals. It's not always easy to do. But you've already taken the first steps, which is more than most do, right?

Most people never bother to sit down and look at their finances. Or to plan a path forward to their goals. The fact that you've read this book means you have the will it takes to get there. So slow and steady. Take one step at a time.

And I know not everyone will be able to implement every recommendation. I know I'd be better off financially right now if I moved to some small town where I could buy a house for $40,000. But I have family that needs me nearby, so I take that hit for the time being.

Do what you can. And keep an eye out for creative solutions. The ones I've listed here aren't the only ones. And the world is changing so rapidly that new opportunities are presenting themselves every single day. Know what you need and be ready to leap if opportunity presents itself.

Okay, then. Good luck with it.

ABOUT THE AUTHOR

M.L. Humphrey is a former stockbroker with a degree in Economics from Stanford and an MBA from Wharton who has spent close to twenty years as a regulator and consultant in the financial services industry.

You can reach M.L. at mlhumphreywriter@gmail.com or at mlhumphrey.com.